92
Ben   Jackson, Robert B.

        Johnny Bench

JOHNNY BENCH

by Robert B. Jackson

illustrated with photographs

Henry Z. Walck, Inc.   New York

The photographs on pages 18, 21, 24, 36, 38, 44, 49, 53, 55, 57 and 59 were supplied by United Press International. Those on pages 13, 33 and 47 are from Wide World Photos, Inc.

CONTENTS

1

OUT AT SECOND

JOHNNY BENCH tugged the big mask down over his impassive face and crouched low behind the plate, shouting loud encouragement to the Cincinnati pitcher. As Johnny flashed his sign to the mound and then raised his mitt, the man on first took only a short lead. He was one of the best in the league at stealing bases, but he also knew the speed and strength of Johnny's right arm.

When the Red pitcher took a bit too long with his windup, the runner suddenly broke for second. He hoped to steal the base from the pitcher rather than the catcher; and he had a good jump.

JOHNNY BENCH OF THE CINCINNATI REDS.

The pitch was a lazy curve, slower and more difficult than a fast ball for Johnny to handle; and the
batter swung widely to help his teammate. Nevertheless, Johnny quickly one-handed the ball with the
mitt, smoothly snatched it out with his right hand,
and fired a whistling strike down to second from his
crouch.

10

The bullet-like throw beat the charging runner easily as he slid into the second baseman's tag through a swirling cloud of dust. The umpire's arm flashed up immediately and the runner jogged back to his dugout without an argument, brushing his uniform as he went. Johnny Bench had once more turned what might have been a close play into a routine out.

2

THE YOUNG RECEIVER

BORN on December 7, 1947, Johnny Lee Bench grew up in Binger, Oklahoma. Binger is a tiny farming town in west central Oklahoma, about forty miles west of Oklahoma City, surrounded by cotton, wheat and corn fields and an occasional oil well. Fewer than eight hundred people live there; and Johnny tells reporters that Binger can only be found by looking a couple of miles this side of a "Resume Speed" sign.

When Johnny was a boy, his father, who is one-quarter Choctaw Indian, sold natural gas in Binger. Ted Bench had been a semipro catcher as a younger man, good enough to think about going up to the majors at one point. But when an injury and World War II intervened, he became a truck driver and furniture salesman instead. He was determined, however, that his son would someday become a big league receiver in his place.

As a result he began teaching Johnny about catching at an early age. He always stressed holding the ball across the seams for greater speed and accuracy in throwing, and also required Johnny to throw at twice the distance between home plate and second base. This insured precision at the shorter regulation distances. In addition he taught Johnny to throw from the crouch, which is more difficult but faster than taking time to stand.

JOHNNY AND HIS PARENTS ON THE DAY HE WAS NAMED THE NATIONAL LEAGUE'S MOST VALUABLE PLAYER FOR 1970.

Johnny began catching competitively in the Pee-wee League when he was only seven; Little League ball came next; and then high school, where his team won the state Class B championship. He also played on an American Legion team in a neighboring town about this time. Because his high school team had a total of only nine players, he sometimes played at first or third instead of catching; but he never failed to warm up as a catcher to keep his arm in shape.

He also became an excellent pitcher while in high school, compiling a sixteen-and-one record, including several no-hitters. His only loss was a two-hitter that went to the opposition, 2–0, on an error. Johnny had developed into a powerful batter by this time as well, hitting for a blistering .675 average.

Besides his baseball accomplishments at Binger High School, Johnny was an all-state basketball guard. He averaged twenty-three points, seventeen rebounds and thirteen assists per game and was selected an honorable-mention All-American. Equally successful in the classroom, he was an A student and the valedictorian of his class when he graduated in the spring of 1965.

Although seventeen colleges were then offering him athletic scholarships, Johnny chose not to continue his education. After all, he had been telling everyone since second grade that more than anything else he wanted to be a big league ballplayer.

But while first-class catchers are usually in very short supply in the majors, Johnny soon discovered that big league representatives were not exactly beating a path to his door. No team picked him as their first choice in the annual free-agent draft, and many did not even list him as a second selection.

However, Cincinnati had been greatly impressed by Johnny's catching in two Legion games they had scouted, in spite of the fact that he had gone only one for eight at the plate on those days. He became their number-two draft choice and signed with the Reds for a relatively modest bonus shortly afterwards.

They sent him to Tampa in the Class A Florida State League where he played in sixty-eight games during 1965. He got off to a slow start with his bat there, averaging .248, but his catching skills were immediately apparent. When ex-Yankee receiver Yogi Berra saw seventeen-year-old Johnny in action at Tampa, he commented, "He can do it all now."

The following season Johnny was moved to Peninsula, which represents Newport News and Hampton, Virginia, in the Class A Carolina League and was then a Cincinnati farm club. Greatly improving his batting over his Tampa performance, in ninety-eight games he hit .294, drove in sixty-eight runs, and slammed twenty-two homers to set a club record.

Johnny tied for the Carolina League lead in assists with Peninsula during 1966 and is still remembered for the inning in which he cut down three would-be base stealers in a row to retire the side all by himself. But it must be noted that he also committed seventeen errors in his ninety-eight Peninsula games and led the league in that department as well.

These marks were set over only two-thirds of the season because in late July Johnny was promoted to Buffalo in the Class AAA International League, one step below the majors. He had become a great favorite of the fans in Virginia by then, and they gave him a parade to the airport when he left. They also asked that his playing number be retired from active competition to honor him.

But within a few days it was Johnny himself who had to withdraw from the game. Catching with two out in the first inning of his first game for Buffalo, he broke his right thumb on a foul tip. Before he had a chance to come to bat in the International League, he was forced to go on the disabled list.

Johnny went home to rest while his thumb healed;

and it was there, later in the summer, that he nearly lost his life in an automobile accident. While he was driving back from watching a ballgame in Kansas, a car came at him the wrong way on a freeway exit and caused a head-on collision.

Luckily there was a doctor in one of the cars behind Johnny, and he received immediate attention. Even so, at the hospital he required fourteen stitches in his left shoulder and sixteen in his head. He also suffered from a severely bruised hip, although the doctor told him that it probably would have been broken except for his large bones and great strength.

The injuries kept Johnny from playing ball for the rest of the 1966 season, just at a time in his career when he was making rapid progress and showing much promise. There was also a possibility the accident might have slowed him down a bit even after his recovery.

Fortunately, when he reported for spring training in 1967, Johnny was as strong and confident as ever. And, after a characteristically slow start at the plate, he had his finest season thus far. In ninety-eight games with Buffalo he batted .259, hit twenty-three home runs, and once more had sixty-eight RBI's. His defensive work being equally strong, he was named Minor League Player of the Year and selected

JOHNNY TAKES BATTING PRACTICE DURING SPRING TRAINING EARLY
IN HIS PROFESSIONAL CAREER.

as catcher on the 1967 International League All-Star
team.

By midsummer International League fans were
calling Johnny the best young catcher to come along
since Roy Campanella had been at Montreal before
going up to Brooklyn. The Reds' management was
also impressed; and in August of 1967, when Johnny
was only nineteen years old and had less than three
years of experience in the minors, he was called up
to Cincinnati.

3

THE LITTLE GENERAL

NEAR THE END of each baseball season a number of young ballplayers are called up from the minors to their parent clubs for what is called "a cup of coffee." This is a short stay during which they are closely observed by coaches and club officials before being sent back to the minors for further experience the following year.

In contrast, Johnny played in twenty-six games with the Reds at the end of the 1967 season and immediately became their first-string catcher. Since this demoted the three veterans already on the squad, Johnny had a greater problem than most newcomers adjusting to big league ball. "I couldn't help but feel self-conscious," he told an interviewer. "After all I was just a rookie and one of the catchers had been on a couple of All-Star teams and there I was catching ahead of him."

Nineteen-year-old Johnny was also in the difficult position of handling pitchers who were much older and far more experienced than he was. But they quickly came to respect his ability and were much impressed by his unflappable poise and take-charge manner. Before long they were calling him the "Little General" and working effectively with him—or at least as effectively as they ever worked, Cincinnati then being known as a hitting club that was weak in pitching.

Pete Rose was also a great help to Johnny in those lonely first days with Cincinnati. The power-hitting Rose, known for his crew cut, head-first slides and competitive spirit, made a special point of looking out for Johnny; and the pair have become strong friends since then. They are now business partners as well, owning an automobile agency and bowling lanes in Ohio.

Johnny was unable to play the last two games of the 1967 season because his thumb had been split by a foul ball. He says it happened because he was concentrating so hard on being ready to cut down

DAVE BRISTOL, THE REDS' MANAGER FROM 1966 TO 1969, WELCOMES
JOHNNY TO SPRING TRAINING. NOTICE THE COMPARATIVE SIZE OF
THEIR RIGHT HANDS. JOHNNY'S IS SO LARGE HE CAN HOLD SEVEN
BASEBALLS AT ONCE.

a man on first that he failed to keep his hand out
of the way.

Such banged-up fingers and knuckles have been
accepted by most professional catchers over the years

as part of their job; but not by Johnny. He is determined to avoid the lumps and scars on his hands by which longtime catchers are usually recognized. These injuries can often keep receivers out of the lineup for days at a time and can also shorten their careers.

His solution has been to give up the usual two-handed style of catching in favor of a one-handed method that allows him to protect his throwing hand. Instead of catching the ball between a stiff padded mitt on his left hand and his bare right hand, Johnny uses only his left hand encased in a special flexible mitt. This keeps his bare right throwing hand out of danger most of the time.

Older baseball men are apt to have reservations about the reliability of one-handed catching, however; and Johnny did have a reputation for letting low pitches get past him when he first came into the league. But he has worked very hard at correcting this weakness; and these days no one questions his use of the unusual technique.

Another catcher started the 1968 season for Cincinnati, but he was injured in the fifth game. Johnny then took over, and he has been the regular Red backstop ever since.

His defensive work was outstanding from the very

beginning; and seasoned pros like Cub manager Leo Durocher were soon raving about his performance behind the plate. "I've never seen anything like it," Leo is quoted as saying about a one-handed swipe-tag that Johnny put on a Cub who tried to score from second on a single.

As in the past Johnny made a slow start at the plate in 1968, batting eighth in the power-laden Cincinnati order. Then, in early May, he beat both the Dodgers and Giants by driving in runs to break up extra-inning games; and his average began to climb. Soon he was batting seventh in the lineup, and then sixth. Further improvement moved him up to fifth position; and eventually, by his own request as well as performance, he was batting in the important fourth, or clean-up, spot.

The other National League players voted him the second catcher for the All-Star game at midseason; and he continued to play at that level during the second half of the 1968 campaign. Johnny had predicted in the spring that he would bat .270, drive in eighty runs, and hit fifteen homers. Over the year he batted .275, had eighty-two RBI's, and hit exactly fifteen home runs. He also led the league with 942 put-outs and 102 assists.

The self-confident Johnny has never been one to

A SLIDING WILLIE MAYS OF THE SAN FRANCISCO GIANTS IS CLOSE TO THE PLATE IN THIS 1968 PHOTOGRAPH, BUT JOHNNY WAS QUICK ENOUGH TO TAG HIM OUT.

hide his own light; and he had also predicted in the spring that he would become Rookie of the Year in the National League in 1968. (He had not come to bat often enough in 1967 to be classified a second-year man in 1968.) No catcher had ever won the award before, and it was the closest vote since the contest began; but, sure enough, Johnny won over the Mets' lefthanded pitcher, Jerry Koosman, by a single vote.

Neither was Johnny about to undervalue himself at the beginning of the 1969 season when he and the Red front office were unable to agree on salary. He became a holdout and refused to sign a contract until he was eventually able to settle on his own terms, $25,000 for the year. (While this was a large increase over his former salary, Johnny's present goal is far more ambitious. He wants to be the first $100,000 catcher in baseball, and many are convinced that he will make it before long.)

Asked for his batting predictions in the spring of 1969, Johnny based his reply on the fact that he would be playing a second season in the same league for the first time. He had not had a chance to face the same pitchers for two years in a row before. Then, after setting his sights on .280, one hundred RBI's and twenty-five home runs, he exceeded even these expectations in two categories by hitting .293, getting ninety RBI's, and hitting twenty-six homers.

Named the National League catcher for the 1969 All-Star game in Washington, Johnny homered in the second inning with a man on first and singled in the third. Most of the fans who saw Johnny play in that game would agree with Dodger manager Walter Alston who said, "He'll be the All-Star catcher for the next ten years."

The fans also remember Johnny's dramatic defensive play in the spring of 1969 when speedy Lou Brock of the St. Louis Cardinals tried to steal second. Lou, best in the league at stealing in 1966, '67 and '68, had stolen twenty-one consecutive bases since opening day. He never made that twenty-second, however, because Johnny's booming arm caught him with plenty to spare.

4

THE BIG RED MACHINE

THE CINCINNATI RED STOCKINGS were organized in 1869 as the first entirely professional team in baseball; and Cincinnati has belonged to the National League since its beginning in 1876. In all these years there have not been very many big seasons for Red fans to cheer about. At the time Johnny joined the team, the club had won only four league championships—1919, 1939, 1940 and 1961.

Johnny came up from Buffalo in August of 1967, and that year the Reds placed fourth, fourteen and one-half games behind the champion St. Louis Cardinals. In 1968, his first full season as a Red, they finished fourth behind the Cards again, fourteen games out of first place for a net gain of only half a game in the standings.

That fourth-place finish in 1968 was particularly disappointing to Red followers because Cincinnati led the majors that year with a .273 batting average; and hustling Pete Rose clinched the National League batting championship on the last day of the season. But the pitching was weak, a common condition in Cincinnati at the time, and the 1968 Red mound staff gave up an average of 3.56 earned runs per game, the worst Earned Run Average in the league.

The performance of the Red starting pitchers was no stronger than usual in 1969, Johnny's sophomore year with Cincinnati. But Pete Rose won the league batting title on the last day of the season again, and the Cincinnati team batting average was best in the Western Division. (1969 was the first season that the two major leagues were split into Eastern and Western divisions to allow for expansion.)

In spite of the shaky starting pitchers, those big Cincinnati bats and the durable arm of reliever Wayne Granger managed to keep the team a contender for most of the season. The race in the National League West was the tightest of all four divisions; and as late as September 10, the Atlanta Braves, San Francisco Giants, Cincinnati Reds and Los

Angeles Dodgers were all within two games of first place.

The frailness of their starting rotation ultimately caught up with the Reds, however, and they finished third, four games out. It was the Atlanta Braves who represented the West against the East's New York Mets in the October playoffs.

Those Amazing Mets not only defeated Atlanta with ease, they upset the strongly favored Baltimore Orioles in the 1969 World Series; and most fans were still talking about them when the 1970 season opened. But before long it was noticeable that the Mets had lost some of their magic over the winter. The biggest change in the 1970 Amazin's was that their pitching had become less effective; and this shortcoming was eventually to cost them the pennant.

On the other hand, improved pitching turned what had previously been a contender into a winner in the Western Division in 1970, and that club was none other than the formerly good-hit, no-pitch Cincinnati Reds. After all those disappointing seasons the Cincinnati pitching staff came through at last, leading the club to its first pennant since 1961 and only the fifth in the history of the organization.

Even so, there were times when the 1970 season seemed no exception to the past, particularly in regard to sore arms and injuries to pitchers. During April, for example, veteran lefthander Jim Maloney injured a tendon in his heel that put him out of action for most of the season. And even before spring training had started, Jim Merritt, a tall lefthander with Cincinnati's best record in 1969, broke his right elbow by falling off a roof while trying to recover his son's kite.

But Merritt fortunately made a quick recovery and got away to the fastest start of any major-league pitcher in 1970, winning eleven games by the middle of June. And Gary Nolan, a promising young right-hander who had received $65,000 to sign with Cincinnati in 1966 only to be bothered by arm trouble in later seasons, won his first five games of the year.

Jim McGlothlin, another starter, was a righthander who had come over from the California Angels in a winter trade. Highlighting his first spring with Cincinnati was a string of twenty-three scoreless innings in May. There was also a righthanded rookie in the much-improved Red pitching rotation, Wayne Simpson. He reminded many of the Cardinals' Bob Gibson and allowed only seven hits during his first three games in the majors.

Merritt, Nolan, McGlothlin and Simpson had a joint record of sixteen wins and only four losses over

Cincinnati's first twenty-five games of 1970, one of the biggest reasons for the Reds' early dominance of their division. The team ERA then stood at 2.92, third best in the league.

Johnny was calling all these pitches, of course, although "demanding" might be a more accurate word for him. He generally prevails, even when a pitcher tries to shake off his signal. Completely dominating even the toughest veterans (he calls them, and everyone else, "kid"), he once needled a pitcher into throwing harder by catching a fast ball in his bare hand.

In addition to pitchers McGlothlin and Simpson there were other important new faces on the Cincinnati club in 1970. The most significant belonged to a new manager, Sparky Anderson, the youngest pilot in the majors at thirty-six and an immediate success in Cincinnati. Johnny often called him "John McGraw" after the famous manager who led the New York Giants to ten pennants between 1904 and 1924.

Other outstanding Red rookies for 1970 included Dave Concepcion, a young shortstop who started regularly at the beginning of the season; Don Gullett, a nineteen-year-old fireballing lefthanded relief pitcher; and Hal McRae and Bernie Carbo, who were used alternately in left field by Sparky Anderson.

Carbo, the Reds' first choice in 1965 when Johnny was drafted second, had been the leading batter of the American Association at Indianapolis in 1969. His first major-league hit was a home run on opening day in Cincinnati.

The team's established sluggers like Johnny and third baseman Tony Perez were also clearing the fences early in the 1970 season, the Reds slamming back-to-back home runs three times within the first two weeks. First baseman Lee May and Bernie Carbo hit a pair in the opener against Montreal; Tony Perez and Johnny combined against San Diego; and Johnny and Lee May homered in succession against the Giants.

There were three other Cincinnati homers in that same Giant game, including a winning ninth-inning shot by Tony Perez. Four days later the Red batters cracked a total of seven home runs in a single game against the Braves—two by rookie Bernie Carbo and one each by Johnny, Tony Perez, Dave Concepcion, centerfielder Bobby Tolan and two-time batting champion rightfielder Pete Rose. "We got some good boppers," commented manager Anderson to a reporter in a considerable understatement.

This explosive power at the plate in combination with the excellent pitching and backed up by crisp

32

TONY PEREZ GREETS JOHNNY AT THE PLATE AFTER A FIVE-HUNDRED-FOOT HOME RUN AGAINST SAN DIEGO IN JULY, 1970. PEREZ HIMSELF HAD HOMERED EARLIER, AND THE REDS OVERPOWERED THE PADRES, 5–0.

fielding quickly established Cincinnati as the class of their division in 1970. The Reds won fourteen of their first twenty games and were four-and-a-half games in front of the second-place Giants when the season had barely begun. They seemed so strong, well-balanced and tough to beat that the press started calling them the Big Red Machine.

During those first twenty games Johnny made a faster start at the plate than was usual for him, batting .241 and walloping five home runs. In the same period Tony Perez, the Cuban third baseman, was making a remarkable beginning, batting .452 and knocking nine homers. By the middle of May Tony had an average of .394, thirteen homers and thirty-six RBI's. At that point Johnny had quickened his pace to .274, with eleven home runs and thirty-two runs batted in.

Cincinnati then held a five-game lead over the Los Angeles Dodgers; and it began to look as if the Big Red Machine had already locked up first place in the National League West with over four months left to go in the season. In contrast the Chicago Cubs, New York Mets, St. Louis Cardinals and Pittsburgh Pirates were all within three games of first place in the Eastern Division.

Tony Perez blasted his twentieth home run on June 5 against the Mets; and on June 6 Johnny hit his seventeenth, also against New York. The Reds completed a three-game sweep of the World Champions the following day, crushing them 10–2 as Johnny poked his eighteenth homer and drove in five runs.

This gave him a total of fifty-one RBI's as compared to Tony's fifty-nine, Cincinnati being in the unusual but fortunate position of having the two league leaders in both home runs and runs batted in.

Pete Rose had also begun to connect regularly by this time, hitting .500 during the first eight games in June; and the already powerful Red batting order grew even stronger.

Johnny was able to keep a place in the order even when Sparky Anderson was giving him periodic "rests" from the physically demanding job of catching to prolong his career. A versatile player since his high school days, he was able to fill in at all three outfield positions as well as first base during 1970. This allowed him to take a break from catching and still help his club with his bat.

At All-Star time in the middle of July, Tony and Johnny were still one-two in the National League for homers with twenty-nine and twenty-eight. Tony also had the most RBI's, ninety, and Johnny was third in "Ribbies" with seventy-nine. Tony was then hitting .356 and Johnny, .285.

The season now stood at about the halfway mark for Cincinnati. The Big Red Machine had whirred away to a lengthy ten-game lead over the Los Angeles Dodgers and was nineteen games ahead of the third-place Atlanta Braves. The Reds had won sixty-two games while losing only twenty-six for a very high winning percentage of .705. Meanwhile, the race in the Eastern Division was still tight; and Pittsburgh, playing .562 ball, led New York by only a game and a half.

Voting for All-Star positions in 1970 was returned to the fans; and Johnny's total was second only to that of Atlanta superstar Hank Aaron, selected to appear in his nineteenth All-Star game. Red pitching star Jim Merritt also represented the National League, and the game was played in Cincinnati's new Riverfront Stadium. But it was rightfielder Pete Rose who got most of the ink. He barreled into American

JOHNNY IN ACTION BEHIND THE PLATE DURING THE MARTIN LUTHER KING ALL-STAR GAME PLAYED IN LOS ANGELES IN MARCH, 1970. THE BATTER IS CHICAGO CUBS' STAR ERNIE BANKS.

League catcher Ray Fosse in the twelfth inning to score the winning run and give the National League a 5–4 victory.

Johnny's turn came on July 26 during a game in which the Reds made it three in a row over the Cardinals. He pounded three home runs and also singled, driving in a total of seven runs. This brought his average back over the three-hundred mark to .302, put him in the league lead for home runs with thirty-three, and also gave him the most RBI's in the league, ninety-five. Afterwards he told a reporter, "I've had better days, but I was only eight years old when I had them," referring to his Little League team back in Oklahoma.

But while Johnny's game continued to improve during the second half of the season, the rest of the Big Red Machine seemed to falter at times. Part of the problem was that the team had gotten so far out in front of the rest of the division, there was little challenge left. The Reds' new Riverfront Stadium was also thought to be a factor by some because it was larger than Crosley Field, where Cincinnati had played during the first part of the season, making it tougher for the Red batters. Mostly, however, the difficulty was that same old Cincinnati story, pitching troubles.

JOHNNY HAD A BIG DAY AT THE PLATE WHEN THE REDS CRUSHED
THE CARDS, 12–5, ON JULY 26, 1970, BLASTING A HOME RUN
EACH OF HIS FIRST THREE TIMES AT BAT. HE THEN SINGLED ON
HIS FOURTH, BUT WAS OUT TRYING TO STRETCH THE HIT INTO A
DOUBLE. THE PHOTOGRAPH SHOWS HIM HITTING HIS FIRST HOMER.

After compiling a brilliant record of fourteen wins
and only three losses, rookie Wayne Simpson developed an ailing right shoulder at the end of July
and was eventually unable to pitch for the rest of
the season. Reliever Clay Carroll was spiked in the
ankle early in August; and shortly afterwards Jim
McGlothlin, who had already lost three weeks after
being hit on the knee by a batted ball, was cut over

his right eye by a line drive. And although Jim Merritt became the first twenty-game winner in the National League near the end of August, he strained his elbow during the first week of September.

The bat of Tony Perez also cooled off during the second half of the season, but he, Pete Rose and Bobby Tolan finished seventh through ninth (.317, .316, .316) in the league for 1970. This helped compensate for the late-season Red pitching slump, as did Johnny's continuing to slam the long ball in the latter stages of the campaign.

He accumulated forty-five home runs and 148 RBI's over the 1970 season to lead the majors in both departments, nearly doubling his production of 1969, yet hitting for the same average, .293. Tony and he were second and third to Willie McCovey of the Giants in slugging (total number of bases divided by times at bat) with averages of .589 and .587.

But Cincinnati was able to win only forty games after the All-Star game as compared to sixty-two before it. And they dropped three straight to the last-place San Diego Padres and split with Houston before backing into the pennant on September 17 when the Astros eliminated the Dodgers from the race. Nevertheless, the Reds had been in first place every day of the season except one in April and finished fourteen and one-half games ahead of second-place Los Angeles. Johnny had predicted during July, "When the leaves turn brown, the Big Red Machine will still be around," and he was certainly proved correct.

5

"HAVE A GOOD WINTER"

AFTER THE REDS had been assured of their divisional championship, they still had to wait to see whom they would meet from the Eastern Division in the league playoffs. The Pittsburgh Pirates, Chicago Cubs and New York Mets had been battling within only a few games of each other since before the All-Star game; but none of the three had been able to play well enough to take advantage of the others' mistakes. Some writers even went so far as to call it "the pennant nobody wanted."

But when the World Champion Mets sagged badly enough to lose six out of seven games to the Pirates in the last ten days of the season, Pittsburgh finally gained enough advantage to win in the East, beating Chicago by five games and New York by six. Cincinnati and Pittsburgh then met in Pittsburgh on October 3 in the first playoff game.

Gary Nolan, the only member of the Reds' original starting four to avoid injury during the second half of the season, pitched shutout ball for nine innings. He was helped by the fine stop of second baseman Tommy Helms in the third with two on; but, meanwhile, the Red batters were also going scoreless. Then in the tenth, with the score still 0–0, pinch-hitter Ty Cline boomed a triple and came home when Pete Rose singled. Cincinnati first baseman Lee May batted in two more runs, and the Reds had a 3–0 victory.

Jim Merritt, Cincinnati's only twenty-game winner, started the second playoff game. Although he had worked but three innings in the past month because of his elbow injury, he gave up only two hits to Pittsburgh over the first five innings. After he was lifted in the sixth, the Pirates scored one run; but nineteen-year-old Red fastballer Don Gullett then came on to pitch three and one-third hitless innings.

All the while, left-handed centerfielder Bobby Tolan had been mounting a highly effective one-man offense for the Reds. He singled twice, stole second, hit a home run, and scored all three of Cincinnati's runs as the Big Red Machine won again, 3–0.

In the first inning of the third game against the Pirates, Tony Perez and Johnny both homered over the left-field fence, putting Cincinnati ahead, 2–1. But Pittsburgh tied the score in the fifth inning; and Cincinnati was only able to get one more hit, a single, through the seventh.

After thirteen Reds in a row had been retired, Ty Cline pinch-hit again in the eighth and drew a walk. He moved to second when lead-off batter Pete Rose singled. This brought up Bobby Tolan, who continued his heroics from the second game by banging a two-strike pitch into left which scored Cline and gave Cincinnati the 1970 championship of the National League, 3–2.

This set the stage for an encounter between Cincinnati and the American League champions, the Baltimore Orioles, in the 1970 World Series. Baltimore had recovered from its stunning upset by the Mets in the 1969 Series to win the American League's Eastern Division by about the same margin as the Reds and had gone on to crush the Minnesota Twins of the Western Division in three straight playoff games. Called the "Big Bad Birds" by their fans, they came into the Series having won their last four-

JOHNNY TAKES BATTING PRACTICE BEFORE THE OPENING GAME OF THE 1970 WORLD SERIES.

teen games. The two teams appeared so evenly matched to the experts that one said, "They might play all winter before they decide a winner"; and most fans were anticipating one of the best Series in years.

The opening game got under way in Cincinnati on October 10 when Commissioner Bowie Kuhn threw out the first ball to Johnny Bench; and Johnny also made the first put-out of the Series by catching lead-off Oriole Don Buford's pop foul. Gary Nolan had no trouble with the next two Birds, and the Reds came up for their first time at bat.

With one out, Red-hot Bobby Tolan doubled, moving to third when Tony Perez flied to rightfielder Frank Robinson, himself at Cincinnati for many years before being traded to Baltimore. Johnny was next up, and he singled to left on the first pitch, driving in Tolan for the first RBI of the Series and making the score 1–0.

In the third inning, after the sparkling Tolan had walked and stolen second, Lee May clouted one over the left-field fence to give Cincinnati a 3–0 lead. The Big Red Machine seemed to be running as smoothly as ever; but the Big Bad Birds were soon in full flight, also.

Mammoth first baseman Boog Powell, Most Valuable Player in the American League for 1970, homered in the fourth inning with a man on base to bring the score to 3–2. And Bird catcher Elrod Hendricks led off the fifth with another homer to tie the game at 3–3.

The sixth inning then became critical; and fans will be discussing it for many seasons to come. Lee May led off the home half with a screaming liner that Oriole third baseman Brooks Robinson backhanded as it passed him. Still running into foul territory, he somehow turned and threw without looking, all in one quick blur, to beat May by less than a step. This fine defensive play saved at least two runs because the next batter, Bernie Carbo, walked and was advanced to third by Tommy Helms's single.

Pinch-hitter Ty Cline now chopped a high bouncer in front of the plate, and one of the most unusual plays in Series history began. As soon as the ball was hit, Carbo sprinted in from third—only to find umpire Burkhart on the foul-line, his back toward Carbo, making a "fair" call on Cline's bounder.

"I couldn't believe it," Bernie was quoted as saying later. "I came down the line and there was the umpire. I had to push him out of the way and slide at the same time." Hendricks managed to tag the oncoming Carbo with his mitt in spite of the flattened Burkhart between them; and from his prone position in the sandwich the umpire promptly signaled that Bernie was out.

The Reds protested loudly about the controversial decision, of course, because Carbo's run would have

ALL THREE PARTICIPANTS CONTRIBUTED TO THE CONFUSION SUR-
ROUNDING THIS CONTROVERSIAL PLAY IN THE OPENING GAME OF
THE 1970 SERIES. THE SLIDING CARBO NEVER REACHED THE PLATE,
HENDRICKS TAGGED HIM WITHOUT THE BALL, AND THE OBSTRUCTING
UMPIRE COULD NOT SEE THE PLAY.

broken the tie. They were right to the extent that
films later showed Hendricks tagging Carbo with his
mitt and the ball clearly remaining in his other hand.
However, the films also proved that Bernie never
reached the plate with his slide, although he did
touch it later accidentally.

Apparently each of the three participants had made
a mistake; but whatever the call should have been,
Brooks Robinson homered in the next inning, and

47

this gave the Orioles a narrow 4–3 victory. Disregarding such headlines as "Big Blue Blunder Beats Big Red Machine," Sparky Anderson told the press afterwards, "The umpires didn't beat us. Baltimore did."

But Baltimore had also beaten New York in the first game of the 1969 Series, only to lose the next four to the Mets. ("We have a score to settle," Boog Powell said.) And Cincinnati jumped away to a fast start in the second game of 1970, scoring three runs in the first inning on two Oriole errors, Tony Perez's single, Lee May's double and Hal McRae's bunt.

Bobby Tolan then made it 4–0 with a homer in the third, and further Cincinnati scoring seemed likely when Johnny walked and Lee May rapped a quick shot down the third-base line. But Brooks Robinson made another great stop and started a double play that abruptly ended what might have been a big Red inning.

Oriole bats were heard from shortly afterwards. Jim McGlothlin gave up a towering home run to Boog Powell in the fourth inning and successive singles to Salmon, Buford and Blair in the fifth. When Powell and Brooks Robinson also singled off relief-pitcher Wilcox in the same inning, Cincinnati's lead was quickly gone. Elrod Hendricks next slammed a two-run double that put Baltimore in front, 6–4.

ALWAYS A TOUGH COMPETITOR, JOHNNY CLIMBS THE FENCE IN A
VAIN ATTEMPT TO CATCH A FOUL FLY DURING THE SECOND GAME
OF THE 1970 SERIES.

Johnny homered in the sixth inning, closing the
gap to 6–5, but otherwise the Bird relievers stalled
the Machine for the rest of the game. The happy
Orioles thus won their second one-run Series contest
in a row; and the teams moved to Baltimore.

Cincinnati made another good start in the third game when Pete Rose led off with a single and dependable Bobby Tolan reached on a bunt. But Tony Perez bounced to Brooks Robinson, who stepped on third and fired to first for another double play that badly hurt the Reds. Johnny was up next, and he crunched a liner to left that was grabbed by—who else?—Brooks Robinson for the third out. (Sparky Anderson later said to reporters, "I'm afraid to drop my sandwich in the clubhouse. Robinson might dart in and pick it up.")

When Brooks came to the plate in the bottom half of the inning, the Orioles had already loaded the bases against shaky Cincinnati pitching. Starring on offense as well as defense, Brooks doubled to left and drove in two runs.

Cincinnati got one run back in the second, but was never really in contention after that. Baltimore kept widening the difference as Frank Robinson and Don Buford homered, Brooks Robinson doubled *again* and, such was the state of Red pitching, Oriole pitcher Dave McNally surprised even himself by hitting a grand-slam home run in the sixth inning. The final score was 9–3, and the Birds had now won seventeen straight, six in a row during post-season competition.

The Reds were disheartened, of course, Johnny included. Although he had a perfect fielding average in the Series and had made a fine throw to catch Paul Blair stealing in the third game, he had batted only .182 thus far. And just when it looked as if he had a certain hit in the sixth inning of the third game, Brooks Robinson made an almost magical diving, sliding catch of his low liner for the best play of the Series. After the game Johnny did not feel like being photographed, and as he passed a TV camera on his way into the clubhouse he took off his shirt and hung it over the lens.

Most of the fourth game was equally depressing for Cincinnati rooters. Brooks Robinson had a perfect day at bat for one thing, getting four hits (including a home run) and two RBI's. Oriole pitcher Jim Palmer was also tough, allowing only five hits over the first seven innings. Going into the eighth, Baltimore led, 5–3; and there were only six outs between the Reds and a four-game Series sweep by Baltimore.

But Tony Perez, who had been having a poor Series at the plate, led off the eighth with a walk. Johnny then singled into the left-field corner, and two were aboard. Baltimore brought in a new pitcher at that point; and on his first pitch Lee May blasted a three-run homer that put the Reds ahead, 6–5.

When Cincinnati reliever Clay Carroll only allowed one Oriole single (to Brooks Robinson) for the rest of the game, the elated Reds had a Series victory at last.

Although one more Baltimore win would eliminate Cincinnati, the ever-optimistic Pete Rose shouted "See you tomorrow!" to Oriole manager Earl Weaver before the fifth game. Putting action to his words, he doubled in the first inning, whereupon Johnny brought his Series average to .250 by singling to right center and scoring Pete. Lee May and Hal McRae followed with successive doubles, and Cincinnati was away to a fast 3–0 lead.

The Cincinnati attack floundered from then on, however. Even worse, an uncertain parade of six Red pitchers gave up a total of fifteen hits and nine runs to Baltimore. The Orioles dominated that final game, 9–3, to win the sixty-seventh World Series; and the five-contest meeting of the two clubs was pretty much symbolized by one play in the ninth inning of the fifth game. As Johnny pulled a hot line drive past third, Brooks Robinson made a superb diving catch to steal a hit from him for the third time.

And so there was little more the Red players could do in 1970 but bid each other the traditional base-ball farewell, "Have a good winter," and return to

ORIOLE THIRD BASEMAN BROOKS ROBINSON WAS TAGGED OUT BY
JOHNNY IN THIS PLAY AT THE PLATE, BUT OTHERWISE HE COM-
PLETELY DOMINATED THE 1970 SERIES.

their homes. But they were a spirited young club
with a promising future; and Johnny spoke for all of
them when he said, "I hope we can come back and
play the Orioles next year. I also hope Brooks Robinson has retired by then."

6

THE SWINGER FROM BINGER

Johnny did have a good winter and a busy one as well. He received a long list of honors and awards, ranging from being nominated as Best Dressed Athlete of 1970 by the Tailors Guild to being selected Baseball Player of the Year at an Academy-Award-style banquet held by professional baseball during its winter meetings.

More significantly, he was chosen catcher of the 1970 Gold Glove All-Star Fielding Team and named Player of the Year by *The Sporting News,* baseball's most authoritative publication. Most important of all, he was voted the National League's Most Valuable Player by a committee of baseball writers.

The Most Valuable Player vote for Johnny was nearly unanimous, only two writers not voting him first and they picked him second. At twenty-two Johnny became the youngest player ever to have received this award and only the fourth catcher. He was now officially of the same rank as Gabby Hartnett, Ernie Lombardi and Roy Campanella.

All these awards, plus Johnny's considerable natural skill at handling public appearances, kept him active on the banquet circuit in the off-season. Then, too, there were television shows, Johnny Bench

AMONG JOHNNY'S SEVERAL NON-BASEBALL TV APPEARANCES DURING 1970 WAS HIS ACTING DEBUT ON "MISSION IMPOSSIBLE."

Day back in Binger, the December tour of South Vietnam with Bob Hope, and two weeks of active duty with the Army as a cook's helper.

In previous winters Johnny has been known for his dunk shot on a basketball team of Reds led by Pete Rose. His hectic schedule in 1970–1971 did not allow much time for basketball, however; and this probably made Manager Anderson happy because he does not approve of court activity for his players. (Sparky's objections to basketball were more than justified in January of 1971 when Bobby Tolan tore a tendon in his heel. The injury was then reported as likely to keep him out of the line-up until June.)

Another of Johnny's spare-time activities is singing, and he made his professional debut in a Cincinnati night club in 1970. A fan of "middle of the road" rock as well as country and western music, he says his musical favorites are Elvis Presley and Simon and Garfunkel.

But baseball's off-season is a short one; and in January Johnny started working out three days a week getting ready for the start of spring training in February. While many another player after having a big year has been slowed by the distractions of the following winter, Johnny has stated his primary ambition as becoming "the greatest catcher ever to

BIG AND TOUGH, JOHNNY GIVES NO QUARTER TO BASE RUNNERS. HERE HE SUCCESSFULLY BLOCKS THE PLATE AND PUTS A CRUNCHING TAG ON THE SPEEDY LOU BROCK.

play the game," and he applies himself accordingly.

Most baseball experts think he has a very good chance of reaching this goal and are already comparing him to the greatest receivers of the past such as Mickey Cochrane of the Philadelphia Athletics and Detroit Tigers, Bill Dickey of the New York Yankees and Gabby Hartnett of the Chicago Cubs. When Johnny asked Ted Williams for an autographed ball during spring training in 1969, Ted's inscription summarized the opinion of many. "To Johnny Bench," he wrote, "a Hall of Famer, for sure."

Big and tough, Johnny is six feet, one inch tall and weighs nearly two hundred pounds. His size gives him great power at the bat and also makes him a better target behind the plate for the Cincinnati pitchers. His teammates sometimes call him "Cork," because they think his large head is shaped like one; but his big right arm and huge hands are much more important. Johnny can hold seven baseballs at once in his throwing hand, and even his left is strong enough to quickly crease the old-fashioned stiff mitt that he formerly used while catching in the traditional two-handed style.

There are some who think Johnny's ego is as large as his hands, but when he boasts "I can throw out any base runner alive," he exaggerates very little. Besides, as he told another reporter, "If you aren't cocky as a catcher, you aren't doing your job."

HIGHLY POPULAR WITH THE FANS, JOHNNY SPENDS AS MUCH TIME AS HE CAN SIGNING AUTOGRAPHS FOR "BENCH'S BUNCH."

Affable and outgoing, he gets along easily with most players, the press and his numerous fans, known collectively as "Bench's Bunch." "Johnny will come up to you for the first time and it's like you've known him forever," a former teammate commented. He is especially aware of his responsibility to his younger followers. "I still remember when I was a kid and how impressionable I was. I guess that's why I always try to do things exactly right, particularly when we're taking infield practice," he once said to an interviewer.

Most observers have already agreed that Johnny did nearly everything "exactly right" during the season of 1970. His reaction to their praise was "I just hope they're saying the same things about me ten years from now." Bench's Bunch are certain they will.